Marginalia

Doreen Hinchliffe

Stairwell Books //

Published by Stairwell Books
161 Lowther Street
York, YO31 7LZ

www.stairwellbooks.co.uk
@stairwellbooks

Marginalia © 2023 Doreen Hinchliffe and Stairwell Books

All rights reserved. No part of this publication may be reproduced, stored in or introduced into a retrieval system, or transmitted, in any form, or by any means (electronic, mechanical, photocopying, recording, e-book or otherwise) without the prior written permission of the author.

The moral rights of the author have been asserted.

ISBN: 978-1-913432-77-5

Also by Doreen Hinchliffe

<u>Poetry Collections</u>
Dark Italics Indigo Dreams Publishing, 2017
Substantial Ghosts Oversteps Books, 2020

<u>Novel</u>
Sarabande in Blue Blossom Spring Publishing, 2020

For Lin,
    with thanks for over forty years of friendship.

Table of Contents

Margins	1
A Table in the Sun	2
What Lies Beneath	3
Lost at Sea	4
Disused Farm in Autumn	6
In Manor House Gardens	7
Coastal Funeral	8
Images that Cling	9
Abracadabra	10
Open Sesame...	11
Handiwork	12
Namesake	14
The Girl Who Shares My Name	15
Rain in October	16
Love Song of a Sixties Tape Recorder	17
Kaleidoscope	18
Kirkstall Abbey	19
Returning in Summer	20
Seaside Ghosts	21
Timewise (a glosa)	22
Variations on Lines from Goethe's 'The Erlking'	24
Cargoes	25
The Lady Addresses Silvestro	26
The Housekeeper	28
Montmartre	30
Twig	31
Memento Mori	32
An Invitation to Infinity	33
Caliban's Choice	34
Afterwords	36
Prince Hamlet's Ghost	36
Ophelia's Ghost	37
Walking Shadow	38

Security Guard	39
At Iburndale Beck, 1719	40
Holding On	42
Vacant Possession	43
Pluto's Realm	44
In the Wind's Singing	45
Another Country	46
1.	46
2.	46
3.	47
4.	47
5.	48
6.	48
7.	49
8.	49
9.	50
10.	50
11.	51
12.	51
13.	52
14.	52
15.	53

Margins
(after Emily Dickinson)

Sunlight breaks and flickers on the margin
of my book. *Don't read any more*, it whispers.
At the far edge of the page, something is stirring.
It rises like the soft chanting of vespers,
tugs gently on my sleeve and waits.
Although I try to focus on the print,
I'm drawn to what's unseen, unknown. It rests
on the air like louvred light, oblique and slant.
Always show your workings in the margin,
the teacher used to say. Mine seems blank,
and yet reflects an intricate dance. I begin
to wonder if the solid world we think
so real is the distraction. Perhaps it's there,
in the margins, where the meanings are.

A Table in the Sun

A table framed by willows,
flecks of sunlight on a pale blue cloth.
Three empty cups and saucers
perch beside a dark green teapot;
three vacant chairs stand round,
hovering like servants in attendance.
Across the back of one, a scarf is draped.
It hangs casually, seemingly at ease
in the warmth of this August afternoon.
Beyond the lawn, the shuttered house
stands in shade, alone. Whatever guests
there might have been, have gone.

Soon, their tea party will fade
to a faint trace locked in memory,
lost forever, or recalled perhaps,
years hence, as a time of idle chatter,
an hour lazing in the shallow surfaces
that pass for life; or maybe something
deeper will remain, a sense of what
was missed, something that stirred
in the silences between their words
as they leaned back in their chairs
with sunlight flickering on the willows,
and shadows lengthening on the grass.

What Lies Beneath

We're deaf to the lilt and ripple of underwater dark,
the multiplicity of tones that haunt the depths –
legato harmonies and sostenuto symphonies
played out in the black where alien creatures lurk.

The grunts and clicks of soniferous fish,
the plop and suck of fleshy mouths or slap
of luminous tails – all these escape us,
as do the pangs of bells from sunken ships

or soft scintilla chimes of buried silverware
still trapped in wrecks – tureens and tankards,
forks and spoons, washed and pushed by endless
oscillations, clinking forever on the ocean floor.

Though none of us can hear the juddering bass
engendered by the Challenger Deep
(shudder of sudden quake or shifting crater,
clash of icebergs, crack and creak of ice),

some sounds, sequestered through millennia,
are caught by hydrophones and given names –
*the Bloop, the Upsweep, Slowdown,
Train*, the brief recorded *Boom of Julia*,

the *Strange Enigma* off Antarctica, *the Hum,
the Ping, the Whistle*... persistent echoes,
snippets of dissonance, a host of arcane songs
and voices, the source of each unknown.

Lost at Sea

Lone bells
from the sea's depths
toll for him
but no one mourns.
Only his shadow flickers
in the memories
of timeworn fishermen
loitering by the harbour
at the grey close
of a coastal afternoon.

Some recall
how his boat went down
vanished without trace
in a sea
as calm and cobalt
as the midnight sky.
Others remember voices,
lanterns sliding down the sand,
the launch of a rescue craft
that searched for him till dawn.

He lives on
in the margins of minds
finds a space amongst
fading recollections, anecdotes.
A faint spiral of blue smoke
still rises slowly from his pipe
and smells of snuff
waft from a silver box
in the far corner of the bar
he made his own.

On winter nights
his voice can be heard
in the boom of a distant fog horn,
its deep bass drifting
through the windows
of the tiny cottages
as if to warn the sleepers,
reminding them how, long ago,
his universe dissolved in darkness
beneath an ivory voodoo moon.

Disused Farm in Autumn

Out of a dismal sky a swallow dives,
circling fields where, once, tall bales of hay
stood stiff as soldiers. Leaves, like discarded lives,
collect in corners. Rain slants its grey
in puddles on the sodden land, patters
on broken windows. Deserted now, the farm
has only memories to unload. It scatters
them like seeds of grain from a careless palm.
An old barn door exhales a watery sigh,
admits its ghosts. The roof has almost gone.
Only the rafters remain to testify
to days of mirth and milking or what went on
in the loft on summer nights, lit by a June
sun or blessed by the silver scythe of the moon.

In Manor House Gardens

Unperturbed by sultry August heat, sunflowers laze
and lean against the sun, their huge unblinking eyes
tracing patterns of light on the lake, the shifting flecks
of gold that freckle the hands of toddlers feeding ducks.

The wartime shelters tucked beneath the sloping lawns
are long forgotten, though the ice-house still remains.
Once a month, the curious descend its steps to wonder
at the cool chambers of this Victorian refrigerator.

There's a pause as the park falls silent, unveiling its ghosts –
children bowling hoops, girls in lace or boys in sailor suits,
cocky youths with thumbs in braces, city gents in bowlers,
women robed in crinoline with babies in perambulators.

Invading parakeets gatecrash the peace, launching flashes
of emerald across the chestnut's highest branches.
Birdsong resounds through sunlit air and then an antiphon
rises like a hymn, a thousand human voices joining in the fun.

Cries from the children's playground shrink the years.
Everyone's back on a swing again, shouting *higher, higher!*
They whizz down slides and spin on whirligigs,
                                        giddy with pleasure.
Faster, faster! they whoop and holler. *Make it go on forever!*

Coastal Funeral

Along the windswept front
where sky and sea are steely grey
and sudden showers send a trawl
of visitors to gaudy shops
for pac-a-macs and sticks of rock,
a funeral cortege slows and stops.

Two white horses lead.
Restive, they steam and stamp and shake
their long black plumes, drawing a hearse
adorned with wreaths of lilies. A score
of umbrella'd mourners troop behind,
huddled in groups of three or four.

There's an air of sad relief,
as if the person that they mourn
has lived too long, suffered too much.
No fervour marks this final ride.
One woman dabs away a tear,
the rest look solemn, dignified.

I pause to show respect,
bow my head as they move on.
Do they sense me here, I wonder,
a stranger standing beside their pain,
sharing, for a moment, the turning
of the tide, the onslaught of rain.

Images that Cling

The rumble of wheels. A fringed canopy moving
through trees, branches intertwining overhead.

A bed with a pale blue blanket. Chinks of light.
The chitter of swallows in the eaves.

Leaves that tuck themselves in corners
or lie in heaps at the foot of a drystone wall.

A tall wigwam. Feathers down my back.
A chopper made of rubber.

Ruzzler-tuzzlers on the mat, my fingers
thick with Brylcreem from your hair.

The air against my face. Windflowers,
wildflowers, roly-poly down the hill.

Still water in the paddling pool.
It's going to be a scorcher, I hear someone say.

Grey stepping stones. Mud between my toes.
Knee-high grass in a sunlit meadow.

Shadows in the garden, the colour of grieving.
The sense of a door closing, someone leaving.

Abracadabra

Dad stands tall in the back yard,
his hand in mine. Together, we watch
the rise of fleets of stars, their flares
trailing sparks across a vast sea of sky.
I wonder if they've come for earthly treasure,
ask if pirates are lurking in the dark.

No, says dad, lifting me up in his arms.
It's abracadabra – just for us.
I trace the arc of a banana moon,
blink at the mysterious ray of light
that slants across my upturned face, cloaking
my shoulders in a pale shawl of gold.

As if we two alone were all the world,
the night encircles us, holds us fast
in a silence that I know I mustn't break.
The moment lingers on, fusing forever
with the scent of jasmine from a nearby garden
and a whiff of Old Spice from dad's skin.

Open Sesame...

the words hung in the air and lingered,
mingled with the smell of woodsmoke
from the constant fire that crackled
at the foot of the double bed
in which I lay for weeks.

Open Sesame...

my father was reading
from the old red picture book.
What's this one called? I asked, chest heaving.
Ali Baba and the Forty Thieves, he said,
holding the page close to my face.
I remember enormous pots, a hot sun,
dark men in baggy trousers
and the black yawn of a cave.

Open Sesame...

he read as if the magic
invested in these words
would somehow make me well again
and as he read I drifted to sleep,
soothed by the rhythm of his deep voice
rising and falling, rising and falling.

Open Sesame...

words imbued with mystery.
I heard them every time
I woke from fitful sleep
to find him still beside me
propped on pillows.
Who could have known, back then,
how long they would live on
as he murmured them in firelight,
with half-closed eyes.

Handiwork

An old Box-Brownie snap.
I see my five year-old self
stare back, remote as an alien,
handless in a blazer bought to last.

Palms on pinnied hips,
grandma tilts her head
and carefully checks me over,
inspecting her handiwork.

My nose is wrinkled up to block
the smell of fumes still rising
from a wad of orange thermogene
she's thrust against my chest

and manoeuvred into place,
pinning it through the wool
of my vest and the thick-ribbed
cotton of my liberty bodice.

I'm standing straight, waiting
for her fingers to move in rhythm
like a weaver's as she plaits my hair
and ties it up with ribbons.

Soon, she'll drape them across her wrist.
I'll hear them rustle and crackle,
inviting me to choose – bright red,
pale yellow, striped or checked.

This faded picture has preserved
her hands, the knuckles cracked and raw
from years of scrubbing, the antlered
veins bulging, blue as bruises.

Smoothing the photo, I touch her thumb,
the one I'd hold and rub with my own
as I went to sleep; beneath the creases
time has grown, I feel her flesh, still warm. ⚏

Namesake

Today would have been your birthday,
your one hundredth, to be precise.
Born ten minutes after my mother,
you were always the strong one, the boss.
You crawled, walked, talked first,
my mother tottering in your shadow.

When grandma decided to clean the curtains
and rip out all the old red felt
behind the pelmet, you were only three.
She smiled as dust-clouds
billowed round your curls.
Diptheria followed – your death
spring-cleaning's side-effect.

Grandma rocked you as you choked.
Even as she heard
the final rattle in your throat
she still held on to you,
sure that the warmth of her arms
could stop you turning cold.

Years later she would sing me to sleep –
Three Green Bonnets every night,
with red on her hands
and dust clouds in her eyes,
and as she sang
I could hear you calling
deep inside her, calling
from a strange and lonely place
that I didn't understand.

Three Green Bonnets is a Victorian ballad about three little girls, one of whom, Dorothy May, is *peeped at* from a distance by the angels and finally *taken* by them.

The Girl Who Shares My Name

Sometimes I hear your footsteps on the stairs
as you clamber up, seeking a yellow room
where a floorboard creaks and the gap between
the curtains still lets in the eye of the moon.

I feel your face brushing against my cheek,
your curious little fingers stroking my side,
as if you've forgotten what it was like to be here,
to lie in a bed in the dark, warm and alive.

Sometimes I see you standing in a doorway,
shuffling from foot to foot like an old clockwork
toy, puzzled by why you've been wound up
then left to run out of breath. I watch you walk

unsteadily towards me, your tiny legs
still mastering the art you barely learned
before you died. You raise your arms, open
both your hands and wait. The no man's land

that stretches out between us melts away
in the fierce light of your almond eyes. Perhaps
you know I keep that lock of hair bequeathed
to me by grandmother. Or maybe you hope

to catch a glimpse of the sepia photograph
of you and my mother sitting in the sun,
that's labelled simply, *The Twins*. I raise my head
and meet your gaze, two disparate lives now one. ⁄⁄

Rain in October

Today thick cloud, the spatter
of rain, and boredom.
I skim the Sunday papers, run
my fingers through the dust that clings
between the keys of my piano, stand
for hours at the window, stare vacantly
at the torrent spurting
                from a nearby gutter.

October, I mutter,
                and the word restores
my first clear memory of autumn.
Back then, as well, rain fell
from skies as grey as guns and gushed
from gutters onto layers of sodden leaves,
their faces streaked with dirt and flattened
                with the weight of water.

I brave the floods,
                don anorak and boots,
trudge aimlessly along the lane
and find myself a child again
listening to the squelch of footsteps in the mud,
the patter of a downpour on my hood,
the constant plop and splash
                from branches overhead.

Beyond the tractor shed
                and the line of beeches,
out there in the open field,
I pause to let the raindrops fall ice-cold
against my outstretched hands
and feel, exactly as I did at nine, the pain
of untold loves and griefs
                and dark unspoken dreads.

Love Song of a Sixties Tape Recorder

Remember how you'd lean forward to touch me,
whispering thoughts, unfolding secrets,
your mouth pressed close to my dark microphone.

You'd read aloud; I'd turn my spools to your
seductive music... *it had a dying fall.*
Music, moody food of us that trade in love.

Shakespeare soon gave way to Tennyson
and then he, too, was *lost evermore in the main.*
Thumb and finger pressed against my volume

you'd experiment with accents, taking all
the parts in *The Wesker Trilogy*, posturing like
Olivier, playing Gielgud to my Grundig.

Where have you gone, my adolescent friend?
Where are all your memories and dreams?
Buried amongst my reels in long-forgotten boxes

or still here, perhaps, in the dust of slanting sunbeams?
If anything might rouse you, wake you now
(how did it go?) *the kind old sun will know.*

Kaleidoscope

(an extended 'gram of &' poem after Terrance Hayes)

You'll find me in the attic under a pile
of toys. First, remove the dust from my pale
blue body, restore my sheen, then slide
your fingers down my smooth sleek side.
Remember how I used to be your idol,
how you held me tight and let me lead
you far away. It's not too late. Pick
me up, gaze on every coloured speck
and marvel at your secret Pleiades
revolving in the dark. Recall how reds
were sparks of fire, blues the eyes of pookas
peering through the woods, greens the polka
dots on your summer dress, yellows pieces
of gold dust falling from the sun. Space
and time have kept us apart too long. Please,
don't put me down. Don't let me be eclipsed.
Don't let fifty further years elapse
before we meet again. I opalesce
for you alone. Come with me. Let's escape,
create new worlds. Nothing's beyond my scope.

Kirkstall Abbey

Pretending to be dead,
I lay stock still in a stone coffin,
clasping my hands in a prayerful pose
and wondering what it must be like
to be a monk deceased, encased in rock.

The abbey was my playground,
the thick black stones of its ruins
my climbing frame, its tunnels echo chambers
where I yelled long lists of abbots – Turgisius,
Hugh Mikelay, Gilbert of Cotes, Robin Killenbeck.

Crumbling walls invited me
to clamber up and sit astride
the narrow gaps where traceried windows
once bore witness to Gregorian chant
or cast slant light on vespers, compline.

To the distant sound of the river
rushing down the weir, I scuttled
through the broken arches of the library
and down a narrow passage to squeeze inside
the domed chamber of my own secret cell.

Here, nose pressed to vellum, I sharpened
my goose quill by medieval moonlight
or dipped my brush in paints with names
that shone like jewels on a dark sea –
malachite, vermilion, lapis lazuli.

Returning in Summer

It's always bitter sweet.
I slip into the northern twang,
taste again the salt tang of its vowels,
the kick of consonants hard as granite.
Echoes rise from cobbled streets
where yacking tongues still blather,
seeking to set the world to rights
between the back-to-backs.

The moors are massaged by light.
An easterly wind sweeps across
gorse and heather, flattening
the face of the grass. I watch it comb
the fleeces of curly-horned sheep
that have grazed on the hillside
for generations and now huddle together
in the shadow of a drystone wall.

Midges gather at dusk.
They swarm round street-lamps,
rising in spirals like the smoke
that swirled around my youth.
I catch a sudden whiff of Woodbines,
steaming coffee in the Wimpy,
the dank scent of mushrooms
picked in early autumn mist.

Dawn restores the long-forgotten
sound of distant hooves on stone.
I hear the slow clip-clop of time
beneath my window and see again
the old familiar childhood horse
that plods across the centuries,
the rags and bones of memories
crammed on his ramshackle cart.

Seaside Ghosts

The air is filled with greenness after rain,
the disused pier now lit by a watery sun.
A gusty wind still turns the weather-vane
remembered from my childhood, although not one
of the grand hotels that lined the front still stands.
I find a shop that sells old postcards, trawl
through photographs of beach huts, crowded sands,
the funfair with that fortune teller's stall.
Reflected in a mirror, I see myself
hunch over, trying desperately to shrink
the years, discover on some antique shelf
the child I was back then, restore the link
to the thrill of carousel and ice-cream van,
and the long-lost songs of the hurdy-gurdy man.

Timewise (a glosa)

The hour-glass whispers to the lion's roar
The clock-towers tell the gardens day and night
How many errors Time has patience for
How wrong they are in always being right.
                        'Our Bias' – WH Auden.

Time's river is relentless in its flow,
converting yesterday to long ago.
As Jack and Jill go tumbling down the hill
and Humpty Dumpty falls from his high wall,
old Father Time repeats, 'I told you so'.
We sense his hands behind the nursery door,
his pattering feet across that childhood street
where Hickory Dickory Dock first wound the clock.
The church bell tolls as treble voices soar,
the hour-glass whispers to the lion's roar.

Stop all the clocks, said Auden, knowing full well
the clocks, in fact, stop us. Our funeral bell
is in their gift. Death, be it slow or swift,
will come at last, our present fade to past.
From birth, we're bound in Time's bewildering spell.
Chronos controls us, though he's out of sight.
Our ancestors bore witness to his trespass,
devising different ways to track their days –
the sun-dial marks the passing of the light,
the clock-towers tell the gardens day and night.

Destroyer and preserver, Time can snare
each luminous moment – moonlight on a stair
or sunlight on wild heather, trap them forever
in that stream of memory and dream
where darker moments lurk, requiring prayer.
We scan our murky footprints on the shore
and feel the past condemn. We let it cast
long shadows, let it wreathe us in regret
for what we cannot change. Yet we ignore
how many errors Time has patience for.

Time observes us from the margins, keeping
his silent watch even as we're sleeping.
Wiser than clocks, he knows he'll only stop
that day when all the armies run away
and children's laughter drowns the sound of weeping.
Until then, he'll spread his wings for flight,
content to know his end will finally show
those puffed-up crowing cocks and despot clocks
insisting that the world is black and white,
how wrong they are in always being right. ⁄⁄

Variations on Lines from Goethe's 'The Erlking'

Why are we riding so late my father,
so late through the night and the wind?
I need you to tuck me beneath your arm,
to hold me tight and keep me warm.

Why can't I feel I am safe, my father?
I'm scared of the night and the wind.
Why can't I stay in the crook of your arm?
Why do you say there's no need for alarm?

Someone is grasping me tight, my father.
That's why I'm hiding my face.
Why can't you see him gripping my arm?
Why can't you sense that he wishes me harm?

It can't be the mist playing tricks, my father,
this whispering deep in my ear,
I'm writhing and panicking, calling your name
but all that you say is *be quiet, stay calm*.

Why do we streak through the mist, my father,
your blown hair over my mouth?
You speak of *our wonderful games all alone*,
but your hot breath is chilling me down to the bone.

The dry leaves stir in the wind, my father.
Like you, they bring death-in-life.
Though you've left your crown and train at home,
You are the erl-king and I am your own.

Cargoes

You dream of Spanish galleons
and swigging wine in coastal taverns,
of mad March days on windswept sand,
exploring undiscovered lands.

You dream of shores with swaying palms
where peacocks flutter emerald plumes,
or cinnamon suns on sapphire seas
with waves that break in a thousand sighs.

You dream of secret hand-carved treasures
hewn from trees across the ages –
Indian sandalwood, Persian lime,
sweet-scented cedar from Palestine.

I dream of chimneys smearing the sky
and rain-filled clouds of pig-lead grey,
of back-to-backs with leaking gutters
and garden sheds crammed full of clutter.

I dream of bargains, half-price offers,
cheap tin trays, cracked cups and saucers,
of boot fairs, boredom soaked in gin,
and how you'll manage when I'm gone.

I dream of what the future holds
when you're my lead and I'm your gold,
when age has burnt your salt-caked lips
and time has sunk our different ships.

The Lady Addresses Silvestro
after Silvestro Lega's 'The Pergola', 1868.

We are practised in the art of seeming,
how to hide our faces behind a cooling fan,
our figure beneath the truss
and fuss of bodice and dress.
Everything in our lives has order,
everything a time of day.
In summer, for instance,
we always take tea in the pergola at four o'clock.
Why don't you paint us here
at the very moment she arrives?

Concentrate on the way
I hold my body taut at her approach
lest anyone suspect
how fast my heart is beating.
Such passion is unthinkable, I know,
but perhaps you can suggest it
in a sideways glance
or the merest hint of a smile.

Capture her when she pauses,
as always, with the tray of tea
and waits barely out of sight,
giving me time to compose myself,
play mistress to her servant.

Perhaps you can depict how others, too,
are engaged in a game of pretend –
my niece trying to imitate her doll,
arms bent at the elbow, legs stiff and straight,
her mother feigning an interest
by leaning forward, chin in hands,
a vast expanse of boredom fixed
behind the glaze of her eyes.

Notice how the pergola frames us,
protects us from the glare of the sun.
We are all in shade,
even she who brings the tea.
Take care to show
the long line of her jaw, her walnut eyes
and the soft curl in her hair.
Examine the way she stands so tall
beside the cypresses, so resigned and still.

Use all your artist's skill
I beseech you, make her embody
the hidden beauty of forbidden love. ◢

The Housekeeper
after Vilhelm Hammershoi's 'Bedroom'

Tonight, my eyes are drawn to a sliver of moon,
the curve of its blade slicing the sky. The house
is slowly wrapping itself in silence, its fire
no longer blazing in the hearth. Ice
carves intricate patterns on windows and light
flickers from countless stars, some long dead.

I recall old tales of ghosts, how in the dead
of night their spirits walk beneath the moon
in search of a lost past, their footsteps light
as air as they step inside each ancient house
they're doomed to haunt. Shivering in the ice-
cold air, I stir the embers of the fire,

sparking a lost past. I think of a fire-
eating father, gypsy mother, (both dead
and buried long ago), remember that ice-
covered winter in Vienna, how the moon
silvered the frozen lake. For years, this house
is all I've known. I slept beneath the sky-light

in the tiny attic at first, made light
of the fact that it was cold without a fire.
After years in France's slums, a house
like this was welcome. When everyone was dead,
I took control. Sometimes, at full moon,
I imagine myself a statue made of ice

and pose outside in the garden like an ice-
maiden, alone and naked. When the light
of dawn forces me back in, I moon
around for hours, allow the flickering fire
to trigger memories. Last month, a dead
rat on the floor made me think of a house

I lingered in once, a pretty bourgeois house
with staff. The butler served champagne on ice
one night and I saw a mouse by his foot, dead
as a doornail. I laughed as I glided past. Sunlight
striking a mirror conjures up that fire
in Pudding Lane, its flames lapping the moon,

or that Parisian house where I'd watch the light
fire the guillotine's falling blade of ice
and gaze on each dead face, white as the moon. ⁄⁄

Montmartre

after Utrillo's 'Place Saint-Pierre et le Sacré-Coeur de Montmartre'

There's a thin layer of snow.
The street is flecked with early footprints from the boots
of artisans and grocers, hawkers of flour or bakers of dough –
the traders who for years have quietly made their way at dawn,
trudging up the slope to all the backstreet shops and flower stalls,
eking out a living from the things they've made or grown.

A few blurred figures stroll in pairs –
two women linking arms, a couple with a dog,
an elderly father with his daughter. They take the morning air
in their expensive hats, the image of content and calm,
as if they come here every day to reassure themselves, confirm
the world remains exactly as it was and means no harm.

Behind them is the Sacré Coeur,
its tall twin domes pure white against a sky of grey.
The church commands the hill. Inside its walls, two priests confer,
preparing for Mass, while from the campanile a bell is tolled.
Rows of candles stand round every statue, ready to be lit
by worshippers or strangers seeking refuge from the cold.

Time has always ambled here.
Undisturbed by-passing wars, the place preserves
a sense of sanctuary. Turn any corner and you're near
a host of well-kept secrets, a multitude of ghosts. They cast
long shadows, inviting you to wander through a maze of alleyways
and squares. *Walk beside us,* they whisper. *Breathe the dust of*
the past.

Twig
after Alex Katz's *Winter Branch*, 1993.

I give you this frozen twig as a symbol of our love –

it's the wishbone we pull together every Christmas,
the forked antlers of the stag we saw in the snow,
a dowsing rod to divine the wellsprings of tenderness.

Thin and fragile as a finger-bone,
it's the windblown shadow that taps on our window at dawn
waking us softly to the warmth of each other's embrace.

Shake it. Observe the way its tiny flakes of frost
are falling on our shoulders like confetti,
conferring an unexpected winter blessing.

Now hold it close between your heart and mine,
feel it stretch its tips far up into the midnight sky
and like a magic broomstick lift us higher,

ever higher, beyond the watching moon
and cloudless dark's conglomerate of stars
towards the hidden music of the spheres.

Memento Mori
(at an exhibition of Victorian photographs of the dead)

Posed and dressed in Sunday best,
their heads clamped tight in a metal vice,
their bodies propped on stands or chairs,

they stare at us across the years
and fix us with their unreal eyes,
inviting us to think them still alive.

We stare back, return the stony glare
of pallid boys in suits and ties
and girls in confirmation gowns,

the startled gaze of babies cradled
in a sibling's arms or haunted looks
of bloodless tots arranged on parents' laps,

each surrounded by a stern-faced family
and favourite toys, pet dogs or cats.
The relatives look stiff as those they mourn,

as if they've long become inured to death,
their children falling prey to cholera or croup.
Yet closer scrutiny reveals a different truth.

The living are struggling, striving
to maintain a dignified stance. Their fragile
masks are merely surface. Underneath,

a father's rage is caged inside his face,
a mother's grief etched deep behind her eyes.
Death is the same whenever he comes.

The camera never lies.

An Invitation to Infinity
after Yayoi Kusama's *'Infinity Mirrored Room'*

step inside the cave of my imagination
    linger in the darkness of its portals   probe
      the mysteries of its innermost circles

leave the trammels of your body
    as you edge forward slowly   adjusting
      your eyes to the vision   the new reality

float in a universe of tiny lights
    ever-changing colours   glide across
      vast unending seas   connectedness

look up   look down   see how reflections
    mirror more reflections   each enhancing
      an intricate dance across black water

bathe in radiance   lose yourself in a trillion
    flickering stars   a phantasmagoria of shimmer
      embrace infinity   realise you're part of the drama ⫽

Caliban's Choice
after Franz Marc's 'Caliban'

Horror and beauty co-exist in me.
Half man, half monster, I live with a divide
too deep to fathom. Since my mother died,
I lumber over the island, scan the sea
for traces of my kind, but there are none.
I dream of storms, imagine wind and weather
smashing boats against the rocks, and other
creatures swimming here. I give each one
a name. My favourite is a slender form
I call Miranda, who walks at dawn beside
the cliffs. Her beauty stops my breath. I hide
when I see her, fearing I'll do her harm.

The monster in me wants to grab her, snatch
her from her tribe and keep her for my own
pleasure. I could bind her with a chain
and gorge myself on her flesh, just like the witch
who was my mother did with bears and goats
she caught. (Their frantic silhouettes would rise
on the walls of her cave and I'd hear their cries
of anguish as she sank her teeth in their throats.)
The man in me thinks differently. He fears
to touch her, bids me listen to the call
of gulls, the sound of wave-song, wind-song and all
the island's music that hums about my ears.

Trapped in a chasm that splits my soul in two,
I veer between its opposite sides, each
of equal force. Nothing can mend the breach.
Engulfed in darkness, unable to be true
to who I really am, I feel the pull
and power of Sycorax, hear her voice
insisting I must make a final choice
and follow her... and yet, the isle is full
of noises, sounds and sweet airs that give delight,

not hurt. Sometimes, I dream of clouds that break
in gold across the sea at dawn and make
me long to live forever in their light... ⁄⁄

Afterwords
(a pair of 'found' poems from Shakespeare's 'Hamlet')

Prince Hamlet's Ghost
Each word in this sonnet is taken from the Ghost's speech to his son, Hamlet, at the opening of the play.

The scent of morning air within the orchard
was brief, as was the glow-worm's soft, pale fire.
Brief are those thorns that prick and sting the body
and brief the gates and alleys of eager love.
My farewell was instant, my falling-off
a slow decline into a wretch whose soul
was cursed. I let my mind prey on lewdness.
Incest unhouseled me, cut me off
from nature, dignity and custom. Leperous
imperfections barked about my head
and stole my life. Quicksilver swift was my
dispatch, lazar-like. O, remember
that my sins went hand in hand with virtue
and heaven, once, did shape this royal life.

Ophelia's Ghost

*This sonnet is composed entirely of words
taken from Hamlet's four brief speeches
to Ophelia in Act 3, Scene 1.*

You loved me not, though I was chaste as ice
and pure as snow. I never loved another
and yet you would accuse me to my face
of wantonness. What was it that your mother
did to transform your thoughts and make you go
crawling between earth and heaven as if
you were a breeder of monsters? Now, I know
that all my love for you was not enough
to keep you honest. Indifferent you were
to me and so, in time, mad thoughts did shape
my life into your likeness. What and where
and why did plague me. I had but one escape.
No more myself, no more the fool of time,
I heard the force of the beck lisp your name ⧸⧸

Walking Shadow

You notice only what remains of me
the things I keep beside me, close at hand,
a stick, a pipe, a suitcase and a key.

You toss embarrassed coins for cups of tea
or snigger as I shuffle down the Strand –
you notice only what remains of me.

I doze outside the station, head on knee,
and place beside the vacant paper-stand
a stick, a pipe, a suitcase and a key.

I have no face, no name, no family tree,
no past to mourn or future to be planned –
you notice only what remains of me.

I walk in limbo, neither chained nor free,
and carry with me through this no man's land
a stick, a pipe, a suitcase and a key.

One morning, walking by the Thames, you'll see
my body lying prostrate on the sand.
You'll notice only what remains of me –
a stick, a pipe, a suitcase and a key.

Security Guard

My uniform is badgeless,
my boots flecked with the dust
of red bricks from the yard
whose boundaries I patrol by night,
passing time by counting spikes on fences,
measuring borders by the number of my paces.

No questions asked,
they pay me cash in hand,
let me sleep in a shed at the back.
Most afternoons, in *The Builder's Arms*,
I plant myself defiantly at the bar, a stance
I hope will guarantee me space and silence.

Beneath the peak of my cap
my face is half in shadow,
dark and chiselled, the lines etched deep.
My heavy-lidded eyes focus on nothing.
I keep my fists deep in my pockets, my feet
spread wide as if to anchor my frame's dead weight.

My speech, when it comes,
is halting, grudging, monosyllabic.
I'm uneasy, wary of conversation,
shun unwelcome contact of any sort.
Over the years I've grown smaller, more resigned.
Being forced to hide is making me impossible to find.

At Iburndale Beck, 1719

I were warped from birth. *Born afore time,*
ma said, *wi' one arm straight and pointin' down
and t'other bent and twisted up. Nay water
nor scrubbin'* she told me, *can teck away that dark
brown mark on yer neck.* Tongue-tied till risin'
five, I were clumsy, allus gettin' a spell

in mi finger or cuttin' meself. *Tha's been under a spell
o' some sort since tha were born,* pa said. Each time
'e looked at me, 'e cursed. When I were risin'
twelve, 'e sent me wi' mi brother down
t' barn to 'elp wi' milkin'. It were dark
when we got up, and rainin'. I 'eard water

and mud squelchin' under mi boots, water
drippin' onto puddled earth. This spell
o' weather lasted till *they* started – dark
whispers, fingers pointin'. The very first time
I 'eard folk call me 'witch', I were trudgin' down
to barn wi' mi dog, Tess. T'sun were risin'

when five lads come. I saw their 'eads risin'
o'er top o' ridge, not far from water-
well. Tess were growlin' so I med her lie down.
Tha's a witch, they yelled. *Cast a spell
for us with yer familiar. Stop time
on yonder clock or meck the sun go dark.*

Soon, there were talk o' sorcery, o'dark
arts and tricks. They said I'd made the risin'
river flood its banks, that it were time
to flush me out. One day, by t'old water-
mill, a woman said I'd put a spell
on her daughter, made 'er tumble down

some steps and lose 'er bairn. I felt reet down
in dumps for a good while after. It were a dark
Sunday morn they took me. *Where's yer spell-
book?* they said, then trussed me up. Dawn were risin'
as they dragged me out wi' Tess. *Let's water
'er witch's teat,* they chuckled. *It's ducking-time.*

They lowered me down in t' beck. I kept risin'
and fallin', flailin'. Then it were all dark water.
Spell-bound, I felt its blackness swallowin' time. ◊

Holding On

What's for tea? She says it over and over
again, as if unable to live with silence,
as if still anchored to a land where time

makes sense and what she once called home is over
there, within touching distance. The silence
at night scares her, resurrects the time

when everything was all at sea, tossed over-
board, the time she lost her foothold, when silence
drowned her cries. She listens. Her heart beats time,

time after time in the dark. Is the silence over? ⁄⁄

Vacant Possession

this is the place where time has stored our heartbeats
wound us in on the long skein of its years

our scrawled initials lie beneath the surface
thick layers of paint have not concealed our fears

we conjure shadows in the starlit attic
and whisper in the cupboard below the stairs

our breath still rises warm from the cold cellar
misting the broken mirror with our prayers

we scurry down the draughty corridors
and weep behind closed doors so no one hears

our elbows rest on every window-sill
waiting for the moon to dry our tears ⁄⁄

Pluto's Realm

The space between
sleep and waking
is a country not on any map,
a place where thoughts and dreams
coalesce, merge with bric-a-brac
tossed up from distant times –

tar melting on the sticky sole of a sandal,
a powdered clown, black holes for eyes,
his lips curved in a crimson smile,
frosted fields glimpsed from the back of a car,
a monkey money-box swallowing sixpence,
frogspawn shivering in a jar.

This is Pluto's realm,
flickering underworld of images
like shadows on the surface of water,
their outlines trembling, almost touched,
yet fading, already fading,
even as we think them fixed.

In the Wind's Singing
(voices are in the wind's singing – T S Eliot)

The sound of the wind beneath the door
is nothing new, and yet tonight
I feel compelled to listen to its music.

It sings of a rickety stile, a gate that creaks
and fields where blackberries hang in clusters,
meandering over miles of drystone walls.

I hear the drone of far-off bees and bluebottles,
the swish of a butterfly net and a sudden whoosh
of breath, scattering the fuzz on a dandelion clock.

Footsteps echo down a moonlit path
where hedgehogs snuffle in the undergrowth
and the call of a tawny owl bewitches.

Something more than memory is moving
under the whispering cicadas in the wild grass
trailing round the long-abandoned railway track.

Something deeper than history is stirring
in the rhythmic plop of pebbles skimmed on water,
the song of the sea in a beachcombed shell.

Another Country
(a heroic crown of sonnets)

1.

That place I dreamed of, vowed one day I'd find
before it was too late – its name is on
the tip of my tongue, its contours haunt my mind.
Is it a place I made up, a country now gone,
no longer on the map, erased forever
like Burma, Persia, Gold Coast or Siam?
Can I never discover its borders, never
recover who I was or who I am?
Perhaps it was a land of myth, a deep
Atlantis or a misty Shangri-La,
a land I have no hope of waking from sleep
with a tardy kiss, that's always a step too far.
Why, then, do I go on searching, believing
it's still out there, waiting for me, grieving.

2.

It's still out there, waiting for me, grieving
over something precious, something I lost
in youth. I watch the silver contrails weaving
through the dark, the skitter of leaves tossed
in moonlit wind and catch a hint of what
I seek, a fragment of myself concealed
by shadows of the past. Perhaps it's not
beyond my reach but wants to be revealed.
It thrives in silence and in candlelight,
hovers close when I'm alone. I hear
its whispers as I lie awake at midnight
seeking its source, hoping the mist might clear.
Shrouded in darkness, it's like an ancient rune
yearning for the spotlight of the moon.

3.

Yearning for the spotlight of the moon,
I walk the woods in darkness. Wet leaves wrap
themselves around my feet. Branches tap
their secret morse in the rising wind. Soon,
the witching hour will toss up scraps of my past,
memories of childhood – fears of the night
and its many shadows, the way the eerie light
of dawn filtered through the curtains and cast
a grey streak on the wall. I let my mind
wander as it will, hoping I'll somehow
resurrect what's lost, retrieve the key
to that strange country I can never find.
I know it's close. I sense it, here and now.
Like some abandoned ghost, it follows me.

4.

Like some abandoned ghost, it follows me,
seeking to unite me with the might-
have-been or that first self who travelled light,
unburdened by the weight of time and free
from all the rigmarole of age, where knots
proliferate, each one tightened by
the next, until there's no discovering why
you're inextricably enmeshed. What's
gone is past. There's no going back. And yet
my secret country wants just this. It seems
to sing, sometimes, from seas where corals lie
in purple clusters, weaving a delicate net
across the deep. At other times, in dreams,
it calls me in the distant ocean's sigh.

5.

It calls me in the distant ocean's sigh,
whispering of some long-abandoned ground
where feathery fountain grasses grow waist-high
and clumps of knotweed wind themselves around
the self I've lost, the paths I never took.
How can I reach a land that's just a ghost
on the unturned page of a forgotten book?
How can I chart its sea, the line of its coast?
I can't stop searching, can't halt the tantalising
spell bewitching me. No matter where
I go, its plaintive call returns. Rising
on the wind, it carries, borne on the air
like the hoot of an owl or a vixen's bark
on winter nights, in the restless sleepless dark.

6.

On winter nights, in the restless sleepless dark,
my mind revolves round images replayed
across a starless sky. Some are stark
reminders of blunders, turnings missed or made
in error. Others rise from the hidden places
I shrink from visiting, yet feel I must,
as though rewinding time will heal. Faces
flicker. The pain of the past sheds its dust.
I burrow under pillows, let my mind
go blank. The world is still and silent then,
my breathing soft and even. As thoughts unwind,
I sense another country, hear again
the voice that seeks a different, deeper me.
Its song is always mournful, minor key.

7.

Its song is always mournful, minor key,
a ground-bass weaving under sleep, the sound
of its insistent rhythms wrapped around
my breathing and half-heard, like a far-off sea.
The music makes me think of mythic lands –
Arcadia and Avalon, Annwn
and Thule or hidden regions yet unknown
that lie in Arctic ice or desert sands.
Earth and air conspire to keep me guessing,
intrigue me, draw me in. My intellect
attempts to crack the maze with language, detect
some logic, but I end up reassessing
words. Perhaps they're futile in this search,
like plainsong echoing round an empty church.

8.

Like plainsong echoing round an empty church
my words reverberate inside my head
and fade, leading nowhere. Is it dead
and lost forever, the land that prompts my search,
or else, through powers not yet understood,
does it somehow still exist out there?
Perhaps the mystery is not at all
unlike those flowers I used to love in childhood –
fern ragwort that was found on every verge,
summer lady's tresses whose flowers would grow
in spirals, small bur parsley, purple surge
and delicate ghost orchid. Although I know
each flower is near extinct, its fragrance spent,
sometimes I catch a half-remembered scent.

9.

Sometimes I catch a half-remembered scent
as past and present merge. Dank leaves evoke
an autumn walk, first conkers, a steep descent
through arching trees. The smell of acrid smoke
restores the taste of fog in my throat, a light
in a toyshop window, my father's hand in mine.
Fragrance of pine calls up that winter night
with fireworks, our final Auld Lang Syne.
Time present and time departed. The flux
of time encircles and defeats us. There's no
escaping the endless tick of 'now' that sucks
us under, no way but death to halt its flow.
Why then do I long for what can't last,
a faint glimpse of my lost land from the past?

10.

A faint glimpse of my lost land from the past
is what I'm looking for, with no real hope
of ever finding. I follow shadows cast
across my life by a chimera, grope
my way towards a meaning that may lie
so far from reach I'll never navigate
its seas or fathom its depths. I'm tired of why
and wherefore. Maybe I should stop and wait.
Perhaps it will appear some moment when
it's least expected. It will be like a trick
of the light at first, advancing slowly. Then,
when it comes, it will be sudden, as quick
as summer lightning, hard to be denied,
sweeping me up in a rush of surging tide.

11.

Sweeping me up in a rush of surging tide
is how I long for it to come, surprising
in its suddenness. I'll watch it rising
through mist, see it dissolve the fog and glide
nearer, overwhelming in its sheer
intensity, uniting us at last
and recreating moments from my past
I thought long gone – the moment by the weir
when stars tumbled down the water, the night
the moon followed me home surrounded by
a star-Armada, the time the peacock fanned
his turquoise for me, his feathers flecked with light.
In such dreams, my land's no longer shy –
it wraps me in the warmth of pure white sand.

12.

It wraps me in the warmth of pure white sand
as if I were a long-lost child, now found.
Yet such imaginings are no firm ground
for hope or for belief. My secret land
might be an actual place, or just fool's gold;
or maybe both at once, like Schrödinger's cat?
Modern science teaches caution. The spat
between the physicists goes on. We're told
that Newton's clockwork universe won't chime
with random atoms. Certainty reigns no more.
Only probabilities exist.
The world emerged from sub-atomic mist,
yet looks, to us, so solid and so sure,
as if it had been there from the dawn of time.

13.

As if it had been there from the dawn of time,
the world deceives us with its certainties.
Laws of nature govern its rhythm and rhyme
within set rules; and yet, uncertainties
abound. Quixotic quanta's complex dance
has made materialism obsolete,
the world no longer closed but subject to chance.
It's clear that dice and destiny must meet.
Paradox drives the cosmos. Free will is mixed
with fate, matter less solid than it seems.
Determinism bound us; now nothing's fixed
but open to possibilities and dreams;
so could it be there waiting, my lost land,
waiting for my footsteps, the touch of my hand?

14.

Waiting for my footsteps, the touch of my hand,
it's nearer than the eye and yet more distant
than the stars. Who can understand
the paradoxes at its heart – the constant
flickering of slant light across a shoulder
in the darkest of places, dispelling fears,
the harmonies so strange and new, yet older
than the ancient music of the spheres?
The land I long for I have often thought
unreachable. Desperate to resolve
its mysteries, I've followed shadows, caught
at traces. Will the mists finally dissolve?
Will it unveil itself to conscious mind,
that place I dreamed of, vowed one day I'd find?

15.

That place I dreamed of, vowed one day I'd find;
it's still out there, waiting for me, grieving,
yearning for the spotlight of the moon.
Like some abandoned ghost, it follows me.
It calls me in the distant ocean's sigh
on winter nights in the restless, sleepless dark.
Its song is always mournful, minor key,
like plainsong echoing round an empty church.
Sometimes, I catch a half-remembered scent,
a faint glimpse of my lost land from the past.
Sweeping me up in a rush of surging tide,
it wraps me in the warmth of pure white sand,
as if it had been there since the dawn of time,
waiting for my footsteps, the touch of my hand. ⁄⁄

Acknowledgements

A number of these poems, or previous versions of them, have appeared in *Acumen, Dream Catcher, Reach Poetry, Sentinel Literary Quarterly, South, The Frogmore Papers* and *Weyfarers*.

Several have also won or been placed in the following competitions:
Acumen International Poetry Competition, 2021.
Ealing Poetry Competition, 2002.
Guernsey 'Poems on the Buses' competition, 2002.
Sentinel Literary Quarterly Competition, 2020.
Slipstream Poetry Competition, 2022.
The Poetry Kit Competition, 2019.
Ware Poetry Competition, 2019, 2020.

Disused Farm in Autumn was shortlisted in Open Poetry's International Sonnet Competition, 2007 and was later published their anthology, *Hand Luggage Only*, edited by Christopher Whitby.

I would like to thank the following people for their help in the compilation of this collection:

Tamar Yoseloff and all the members of her Wednesday evening seminar group for their constructive feedback on work in progress and for their support, advice and encouragement over many years.

The members of Greenwich Poetry Workshop and Greenwich Stanza for lots of inspiring discussions and for their useful comments and suggestions.

Other anthologies and collections available from Stairwell Books

Yorkshire Crabs	F. Mary Callan
The Estuary and the Sea	Jennifer Keevill
In	Between	Angela Arnold
Quiet Flows the Hull	Clint Wastling
Lunch on a Green Ledge	Stella Davis
there is an england	Harry Gallagher
Iconic Tattoo	Richard Harries
Fatherhood	CS Fuqua
Herdsmenization	Ngozi Olivia Osuoha
On the Other Side of the Beach, Light	Daniel Skyle
Words from a Distance	Ed. Amina Alyal, Judi Sissons
Fractured	Shannon O'Neill
Unknown	Anna Rose James, Elizabeth Chadwick Pywell
When We Wake We Think We're Whalers from Eden	Bob Beagrie
Awakening	Richard Harries
Starspin	Graehame Barrasford Young
A Stray Dog, Following	Greg Quiery
Blue Saxophone	Rosemary Palmeira
Steel Tipped Snowflakes 1	Izzy Rhiannon Jones, Becca Miles, Laura Voivodeship
Where the Hares Are	John Gilham
The Glass King	Gary Allen
A Thing of Beauty Is a Joy Forever	Don Walls
Gooseberries	Val Horner
Poetry for the Newly Single 40 Something	Maria Stephenson
Northern Lights	Harry Gallagher
Nothing Is Meant to be Broken	Mark Connors
Heading for the Hills	Gillian Byrom-Smith
Lodestone	Hannah Stone
Unsettled Accounts	Tony Lucas
Learning to Breathe	John Gilham
New Crops from Old Fields	Ed. Oz Hardwick
The Ordinariness of Parrots	Amina Alyal
Homeless	Ed. Ross Raisin
Somewhere Else	Don Walls

For further information please contact rose@stairwellbooks.com

www.stairwellbooks.co.uk
@stairwellbooks

www.ingramcontent.com/pod-product-compliance
Lightning Source LLC
Chambersburg PA
CBHW031215090426

42736CB00009B/929